The Child King
An Advent Devotional

Graceview Baptist Church
Hill Church
South Point Fellowship

The Child King

CONTENTS

INTRODUCTION

The Child King: An Advent Devotional is a collection of 27 daily devotional readings for the Advent season intended to begin four weeks before Christmas and going through Christmas Day. *The Child King* covers the four main themes of Advent (hope, peace, love, and joy), and it ultimately points us toward Christ.

The word *advent* means "coming," and the Advent season is a period of time leading up to Christmas when Christians remember the first coming of Jesus at Christmas and look forward to the second coming of Jesus in the future.

Our hope is that you would be able to read through this devotional each day of this Advent season and be able to see Jesus in a new way leading up to Christmas. Whether you read *The Child King* as an individual, as a couple, or with your kids as a family, our prayer is that your focus this Advent season would be firmly in Christ and the hope, peace, love, and joy He brings us as we wait patiently for Him to come.

WEEK 1 - HOPE

DAY 1

Luke 2:1-7

In those days a decree went out from Caesar Augustus that all the world should be registered. [2] This was the first registration when Quirinius was governor of Syria. [3] And all went to be registered, each to his own town. [4] And Joseph also went up from Galilee, from the town of Nazareth, to Judea, to the city of David, which is called Bethlehem, because he was of the house and lineage of David, [5] to be registered with Mary, his betrothed, who was with child. [6] And while they were there, the time came for her to give birth. [7] And she gave birth to her firstborn son and wrapped him in swaddling cloths and laid him in a manger, because there was no place for them in the inn.

The Long Awaited Hope Arrives

When most people think of hope, they think about something happening. I hope I get a raise, I hope my kids do well in their play, I hope I have a good day today. For most people, hope has for its end a situational outcome and that is the end of it until they hope for something else to happen. For a few thousand years the people of Israel passionately hoped, but their hope was not for something to happen but for someone to come, the Messiah. They were hoping for someone to come who could bring them freedom, and He came but not just for them but for sinners from all the nations.

J.C. Ryle said, *"Our divine Savior really took human nature upon Him, in order to save sinners. He really became a man like ourselves in all things, sin only excepted."*[1]

As Christians our hope is not tied to an event but to a person. The perfect person, Jesus Christ who took on flesh, lived a sinless life, died upon the cross, and raised to life on the third day. Our hope is found in Him this Advent season, and we can have hope in Him today because He truly came.

Reflection Question:

Is your hope found in events that turn out the way that you want them or in the person of Jesus Christ this Advent season?

---

[1] Elliot Ritzema, ed., *300 Quotations and Prayers for Christmas,* Pastorum Series (Lexham Press, 2013).

WEEK 1 - HOPE

DAY 2

Philippians 1:21

For to me to live is Christ, and to die is gain.

The End of Our Hope

Hope is a funny thing. It can make the darkest storm seem bearable – enjoyable even. It can revive the spirit of someone who has hit rock bottom. And yet, there is always that moment just between each hope-filled heartbeat. That moment that allows just the slightest bit of doubt to creep in. Hope, by its nature, is not sure. It may be an anchor, but it is not a rock. Hope has not yet seen what has been promised or hoped for. Hope, as beautiful as it is, will always bear the stain of not knowing.

Paul's words are meant to fill us with hope. *"To live is Christ."* What a wonderful message from the imprisoned apostle. No matter what life brings, Christ is with us. His name is *Immanuel,* after all (cf. Matthew 1:23). Whether we have plenty or not enough, we can be content in all things because of Christ (Philippians 4:12-13). It's the next phrase that means so much more. *"To die is gain."* Paul could have easily said, "to die is Christ." Another beautifully accurate statement. But living in Christ is not the same as dying in Him. Living in Christ is living in hope – living in faith – living with assurance mixed with our finite understanding of what is to come. We do not yet know as we are known (1 Corinthians 13:12). We can only see clearly the shadows of the true glory that is being prepared for us (Hebrews 10:1). Our death in Christ is gain to us when hope finally ends and we see Him face to face. No more doubt. No more struggle. No more wondering. No more hope. Our greatest gain will be in watching hope fade in the light of our Savior.

Reflection Question:

How do we better live our lives showing that death is gain?

WEEK 1 - HOPE

DAY 3

Genesis 3:15

I will put enmity between you and the woman,
 and between your offspring and her offspring;
he shall bruise your head,
 and you shall bruise his heel.

Hope of a Redeemer

When God created everything it was absolutely perfect. The world operated exactly as it should, and there was harmony with God. This was all broken when Adam and Eve disobeyed the Lord's command and ate of the tree. In that single act of disobedience sin and death entered the world and man's relationship with God was disrupted. The harmony was broken, and with it came consequences. Relationship was severed, and unity was no more.

In the midst of all of this tragedy, God had a plan! This plan was to bring His people back into right relationship with Him. To bring everything back into harmony. To restore unity and conquer death. The very first mention of a Savior who would reverse what happened at the fall is in Genesis 3:15. The snake will attack and bruise the heal of God's chosen people. But one day the Redeemer will come, and He will bruise the head of the snake. Completely crushing him!

Although sin entered the world, there will be someone sent by God, born of a woman, who will restore everything! This is great news! In the Old Testament scriptures God's people looked for the One to come that is first mentioned in Genesis 3:15. The long awaited Redeemer, the One God's people waited on, was Jesus! He is the hope of the world!

The Lord's people had to wait on Him for a very long time. In perspective our waiting is nothing compared to this. Is it hard for you to wait on the Lord?

Reflection Question:

How encouraging is it that in the darkest of that day, right from the beginning, God had a plan?

WEEK 1 - HOPE

DAY 4

2 Corinthians 4:6, 16-18; 12:9

For God, who said, "Let light shine out of darkness," has shone in our hearts to give the light of the knowledge of the glory of God in the face of Jesus Christ.

So we do not lose heart. Though our outer self is wasting away, our inner self is being renewed day by day. 17 For this light momentary affliction is preparing for us an eternal weight of glory beyond all comparison, 18 as we look not to the things that are seen but to the things that are unseen. For the things that are seen are transient, but the things that are unseen are eternal.

But he said to me, "My grace is sufficient for you, for my power is made perfect in weakness." Therefore I will boast all the more gladly of my weaknesses, so that the power of Christ may rest upon me.

The Child King

Hope in the Dark

I'll never forget the first Christmas morning I didn't want to get up. The season, as joyful and wonderful as it could be, had no wonder for me. I had lost someone, and, as the Lord would ordain, I would lose someone else within the month. I didn't want to get up. I didn't want presents or food or family – all the wonderful enjoyments of this special time of year. I wanted what I had lost back. I wanted things as they used to be. I wanted to be happy. I didn't want to be depressed. I didn't want to get up. I was broken. I blamed myself. I blamed the doctors. I blamed God. I cried. I screamed. I ran. He whispered, "*My grace is sufficient.*"

I've lived with depression for 19 years now. I've learned many ways to manage the weight of it. I've learned to battle the thoughts that overwhelm me at times. There are days I still don't want to get up. Paul's words ring truer and truer every day. This struggle is not pointless. It's doing something. The hurt – the struggle – the darkness – is constantly doing something. It's preparing me for the day I will want to get up. It's preparing me for His glory. By God's grace through Christ, there will be no more loss or hurt or depression or grief or darkness. There will just be Jesus, and it will be worth it then. Every minute of our pain will be worth it when we see the light of His face.

Reflection Question:

Memorize 2 Corinthians 4:16-18. Then, when you feel like you don't want to get up, press into the promise of what He's preparing for you.

WEEK 1 - HOPE

DAY 5

Genesis 6:5-8

The Lord saw that the wickedness of man was great in the earth, and that every intention of the thoughts of his heart was only evil continually. 6 And the Lord regretted that he had made man on the earth, and it grieved him to his heart. 7 So the Lord said, "I will blot out man whom I have created from the face of the land, man and animals and creeping things and birds of the heavens, for I am sorry that I have made them." 8 But Noah found favor in the eyes of the Lord.

The Child King

Hope from Judgment

So you are excited to read your Advent Devotional today, you open it up thinking good Christmas thoughts, and BAM! You read some verses about God's judgment and wonder, what does this have to do with Christmas and the coming of Jesus? Well, let me tell you, it has everything to do with Christmas and the coming of Jesus.

Ever since the fall, man has been born with a sin nature, and all mankind's hearts are sinful just as they were in the days of Noah. Since God is just, He judges sin rightly. This is not good for mankind because we are all sinners, yes, even you. No one can stand before God's judgment on their own and be judged other than as a sinner who deserves eternal punishment. This is not good news for any one, but this is where Advent comes in and brings us good news.

You see, in verse 8 of our text today we see that those who are in the favor of God escape judgment, so there is a way to life and freedom. When Jesus came to earth and took on flesh, He came so sinners could be forgiven of their sins and escape the judgment of God. We know that the way for sinful man to be in the favor of God is only through Jesus Christ. If Jesus had not come, we would be without hope, but because He came those who believe in Him alone for their salvation have certain hope!

Reflection Questions:

Is the hope of your salvation from judgment found in Christ alone?
If it is, When was the last time that you thanked God for sending Jesus so you could have that hope?
If it is not, talk to someone today about how you can have your hope in Jesus.

The Child King

WEEK 2 - PEACE

DAY 1

Philippians 4:7; Mark 4:35-41

7 And the peace of God, which surpasses all understanding, will guard your hearts and your minds in Christ Jesus.

35 On that day, when evening had come, he said to them, "Let us go across to the other side." 36 And leaving the crowd, they took him with them in the boat, just as he was. And other boats were with him. 37 And a great windstorm arose, and the waves were breaking into the boat, so that the boat was already filling. 38 But he was in the stern, asleep on the cushion. And they woke him and said to him, "Teacher, do you not care that we are perishing?" 39 And he awoke and rebuked the wind and said to the sea, "Peace! Be still!" And the wind ceased, and there was a great calm. 40 He said to them, "Why are you so afraid? Have you still no faith?" 41 And they were filled with great fear and said to one another, "Who then is this, that even the wind and the sea obey him?"

The Child King

Peace Beyond Understanding

We all have that one friend. The friend who refuses to swim in the ocean after seeing *Jaws*, who avoids clowns at all costs after watching *IT*, who refuses to get on a cruise ship because they've seen *Titanic*. We like to laugh at them sometimes, but we often have those same tendencies. We trust what we have seen or experienced, especially the negative things. We don't want to feel those again, and we will do anything to maintain the delicate peace we have manufactured for ourselves.

The peace that Christ brings is a peace that often asks us to trust Him in the midst of difficult circumstances. Christ commands us to love our enemies, take up our crosses, and rejoice when we are persecuted. He asks us to find our peace in Him, not in our circumstances. The story in Mark chapter 4 gives us a glimpse of how Christ's peace transcends our understanding and experience.

The story opens with Jesus sleeping on a boat while His disciples sail across the sea of Galilee. Then the storm hits. They had heard of storms like this. They had seen storms like this. Some of their fathers were fishermen, and they had been raised hearing stories about these storms. Some of them may have even known someone who was lost in a storm like this one. Fear was the understandable reaction. Peace made no sense in the middle of a storm. And yet, Christ, after rebuking the storm, rebuked them for their lack of faith – their lack of peace. The story of the storm reminds us that our peace is found in Him, not in our circumstances. And His peace goes far beyond our understanding.

Reflection Question:

What are areas in your life where your experience has kept you from walking in the peace of Christ?

WEEK 2 - PEACE

DAY 2

Isaiah 9:6

For to us a child is born,
  to us a son is given;
and the government shall be upon his shoulder,
  and his name shall be called
Wonderful Counselor, Mighty God,
  Everlasting Father, Prince of Peace.

The Prince of Peace

Living in the time we do we can often find ourselves wondering if there could ever be true peace. Tensions are always high, division is everywhere, and governments seem corrupt. We can't watch the news or scroll through social media without encountering turmoil. Either the world is getting more chaotic, or we simply have more access to information. One thing is for certain, everything is not peaceful!

All of the unrest and problems we see in this world are due to sin. It affected every aspect of creation. It affected every relationship. We can and should seek peace, but we must be reminded that ultimate peace is found only in Christ. Everything else will come up short. In John 14:27 Christ said, "Peace I leave with you; my peace I give to you. Not as the world gives do I give to you. Let not your hearts be troubled, neither let them be afraid." You see, we will never find it in governments, leaders, friends, or family. Only in the child that was born, the Savior king, the "Wonderful Counselor, Mighty God, Everlasting Father, Prince of Peace." When we see unrest and lack of peace around us, we should turn to Him.

Reflection Question:

Do you ever think about what true peace actually is?

When you look at the names used in Isaiah 9:6 for the coming Savior, which one is your favorite?

The Child King

WEEK 2 - PEACE

DAY 3

Psalm 39:12

Hear my prayer, O Lord,
and give ear to my cry;
hold not your peace at my tears!
For I am a sojourner with you,
a guest, like all my fathers.

Peace Like a River

One of my favorite hymns is "It is well with my Soul." The opening verse says,

When peace, like a river, attendeth my way,
When sorrows like sea billows roll;
Whatever my lot, Thou hast taught me to say,
It is well, it is well with my soul.

Horatio Spafford penned these words as he sailed over the spot in the ocean where his wife and children had drowned. He was a man who had lost so much, but he understood one thing. The peace he needed could not come from inside himself; it had to come from God. He understood that this peace that came from God would be a comfort for his troubled soul. He understood that when that peace came it would be all that he needed.

In times of trouble many do not turn to God like David does in Psalm 39 or Spafford did on that ship in the middle of the Atlantic ocean. They turn inward instead of upward; they look for peace that does not satisfy instead of looking to the One who can bring peace to their souls. One of the names of Jesus that we see in the Bible is the prince of peace. The reason He is called that is because through His coming to earth, dying on the cross, and raising on the third day He brought sinners to peace with God. The Bible also says that Jesus would send the comforter when He ascended so His people would have peace. In this title we see that the peace we seek in times of trouble is found in Jesus, the One who can bring peace to our souls. When you need peace, look to Jesus.

Reflection Question:

Is there an area of your life today in which you need to look to Jesus for peace?

WEEK 2 - PEACE

DAY 4

Hebrews 1:1-4

Long ago, at many times and in many ways, God spoke to our fathers by the prophets, 2 but in these last days he has spoken to us by his Son, whom he appointed the heir of all things, through whom also he created the world. 3 He is the radiance of the glory of God and the exact imprint of his nature, and he upholds the universe by the word of his power. After making purification for sins, he sat down at the right hand of the Majesty on high, 4 having become as much superior to angels as the name he has inherited is more excellent than theirs.

The Child King

The Sinner's Peace with God

Ephrem the Syrian who lived from 306-373 AD said,

It was not seraphim He sent us, nor yet did cherubim come down among us. There did not come watchers or ministers, but the firstborn to whom they minister. Who can suffice to give thanks that the majesty which is beyond measure is laid in the lowly manger![2]

This early Church Father understood something about the greatness of the One who was born in that manger just three hundred years earlier. He understood that Jesus wasn't an angel, He wasn't just a human man, but He was the Son of God, the One who is without measure. So often, we tend to minimize who Jesus is. At worst, we treat Him like He is just one of us, or at best, kind of like a superhero, who is like us but can do some really powerful things. Neither of these are correct. While Jesus took on flesh, He was at the same time all God and all man, and it had to be that way.

In order for man to be at peace with God, the ultimate sacrifice had to be made. It could not be anything in creation that could bring sinners peace; it had to be One who was not created but begotten, and Jesus was that one. So not only did God plan how sinful man could have peace with Him, He provided the way by sending His Son!

Reflection Question:

How do you see Jesus today: do you see Him as Scripture reveals Him or do you see Him as someone less than the Son of God?

---

[2] Elliot Ritzema, ed., 300 Quotations and Prayers for Christmas, Pastorum Series (Lexham Press, 2013).

WEEK 2 - PEACE

DAY 5

Psalm 27:1-5

The Lord is my light and my salvation;
*   whom shall I fear?*
The Lord is the stronghold of my life;
*   of whom shall I be afraid?*
2 When evildoers assail me
*   to eat up my flesh,*
my adversaries and foes,
*   it is they who stumble and fall.*
3 Though an army encamp against me,
*   my heart shall not fear;*
though war arise against me,
*   yet I will be confident.*
4 One thing have I asked of the Lord,
*   that will I seek after:*
that I may dwell in the house of the Lord
*   all the days of my life,*
to gaze upon the beauty of the Lord
*   and to inquire in his temple.*
5 For he will hide me in his shelter
*   in the day of trouble;*
he will conceal me under the cover of his tent;
*   he will lift me high upon a rock.*

The Child King

The Peace of His Presence

David was a warrior. Much of his adult life was spent at war with someone. Saul, the Moabites, the Amorites, and Absalom topped the list of people who'd like to kill him. Few of us can relate to David when he talks about enemies encamping against us or people actually wanting to see us dead and willing to act on those impulses. But we've all had those moments when our minds are bombarded by lies. We are constantly at war with the voice of our enemy inside our heads. Sometimes that enemy is THE enemy – the devil. Sometimes it's the "old man" – the sinful, selfish nature that clings to us even after our salvation. The battle for what is true rages in our minds and hearts. We feel assailed, surrounded, and helpless against what seems like a never-ending onslaught. Peace seems far away and so does God. We feel alone and abandoned. And if we're not careful, we may start to believe God has left us.

One of the great joys of God's saving work of grace in us is being able to pray with David *All I want is to be with You. All I desire to do is see Your beauty, to feel Your comfort, and be close to You.* When our words align with our lives in seeking Him in His Word and in prayer, our gracious God gladly comes near. And when He is near, those voices that seemed so loud and menacing before are overwhelmed by the peace that only God's presence can bring.

Reflection Question:

What voices bombard you? What truths from God's Word can help you battle those voices?

WEEK 2 - PEACE

DAY 6

Hebrews 12:12-15

Therefore lift your drooping hands and strengthen your weak knees, [13] and make straight paths for your feet, so that what is lame may not be put out of joint but rather be healed. [14] Strive for peace with everyone, and for the holiness without which no one will see the Lord. [15] See to it that no one fails to obtain the grace of God; that no "root of bitterness" springs up and causes trouble, and by it many become defiled.

Live in Peace

The writer of Hebrews reflects back on the Old Testament failure of Esau that we are all familiar with. He missed the mark when it came to "striving for peace," and devastatingly so. In comparison to that the New Testament church is called to not fall into the trap of disunity. As Romans 14:19 says, "So let us pursue what makes for peace and for mutual upbuilding."

We all know that life can truly be a mess sometimes – often of our own doing and on occasion due to the failures of others. Believers are called to "strive for peace with everyone," as the author of Hebrews says. What does this mean? How can we do this? In our own power we cannot. We'll fail over and over again.

But, if we find our peace in Christ, we in turn display that to the world around us. We represent the root of our peace to the people we come into contact with on a daily basis. We show them what it looks like to live the Christian life. So in this let us reflect on the coming of our Savior and pursue peace through the power of Jesus.

Reflection Questions:

What does truly "striving for peace" look like?

How can you pursue this on a daily basis as the Lord continues to sanctify you?

WEEK 2 - PEACE

DAY 7

Colossians 3:12-15

Put on then, as God's chosen ones, holy and beloved, compassionate hearts, kindness, humility, meekness, and patience, [13] bearing with one another and, if one has a complaint against another, forgiving each other; as the Lord has forgiven you, so you also must forgive. [14] And above all these put on love, which binds everything together in perfect harmony. [15] And let the peace of Christ rule in your hearts, to which indeed you were called in one body. And be thankful.

The Peace of Christ

The Apostle Paul tells the church at Colossae that "as God's chosen ones" their lives should have certain characteristics. Compassion, kindness, humility, meekness, and patience are all important marks of believers. The funny thing is he mentions all of these things just before saying "bearing with one another." In other words, relationships will be difficult, and you will need all of the things previously mentioned to handle things in a God honoring way. All of this is wrapped up in putting love above everything and letting peace rule your hearts.

The peace that should rule is the "peace of Christ," Paul says. So during this season as we are reminded of the source of peace, let us also be reminded that the same peace should rule in our lives. When life gets crazy, when we are overwhelmed and fall short, remember that the Prince of Peace has redeemed you. At Christmas time we should reflect upon the Savior that was born to give us a peace that is beyond understanding. More than ever we should express this to everyone around us and let peace rule our hearts!

Reflection Questions:

Is your life an example of the qualities the apostle Paul mentions? Compassion, kindness, humility, meekness, and patience.

How does letting peace rule your heart and bearing with one another tie together?

WEEK 3 - LOVE

DAY 1

Genesis 29:18-20

Jacob loved Rachel. And he said, "I will serve you seven years for your younger daughter Rachel." 19 Laban said, "It is better that I give her to you than that I should give her to any other man; stay with me." 20 So Jacob served seven years for Rachel, and they seemed to him but a few days because of the love he had for her.

The Child King

The Price of Love

In 1989 a little movie was released entitled "Say Anything."
It is the story of first love. Lloyd, an unwavering optimist,
attempts to win the heart of Diane, a girl who seems way out
of his league. Surprisingly to everyone, Diane returns
Lloyd's sentiment, and the two make a connection. Diane's
father does not approve of their relationship and attempts to
pull them apart, and then Lloyd does the unthinkable. He
stands outside of Diane's house and raises his giant boom
box to the heaven and plays Peter Gabriel's song "In your
Eyes." It is a scene that lives in movie infamy and speaks to
the lengths one will go for love.

Now this is a great story, but it pales in comparison to what
Jacob did for Rachael. He served her father for seven years
to be able to marry her. Seven years! If Lloyd's sacrifice was
a two on a scale of one to ten, Jacob's is an eight. He put his
life on hold for seven years instead of seven minutes in order
to win the one he loved. But these stories pale in comparison
to what Christ did for the Church, whom He loves.

Jesus Christ humbled himself, took on flesh, went to the
cross, and died for His bride. There has never been a greater
example of love in the history of mankind than what Jesus
did by taking on flesh and dying for His people. So often we
get wrapped up into love stories, forgetting the greatest one
ever told was for Christ and His Church.

Reflection Question:

As you go about your day today, ponder upon the great love
Christ showed for His Bride, a love that has no measure.

WEEK 3 - LOVE

DAY 2

1 John 4:7-12

Beloved, let us love one another, for love is from God, and whoever loves has been born of God and knows God. ⁸ Anyone who does not love does not know God, because God is love. ⁹ In this the love of God was made manifest among us, that God sent his only Son into the world, so that we might live through him. ¹⁰ In this is love, not that we have loved God but that he loved us and sent his Son to be the propitiation for our sins. ¹¹ Beloved, if God so loved us, we also ought to love one another. ¹² No one has ever seen God; if we love one another, God abides in us and his love is perfected in us.

The Child King

In This Is Love

Our culture consistently defines "love" by feelings. Most often love is expressed to someone or something that makes us feel good or positive about ourselves. It is rare to give love to one who does not give us what we believe we need in return. If we do give love to something that does not reciprocate the positive feelings we want, we reluctantly give love out of some vague sense of duty, obligation, or self-righteousness. God as love is foreign to us. The kind of love that God exemplifies is wholly different than how we love or would like to be loved. Our perception of love is so warped that we want people to love us with selfish motives. We want them to owe us, and we don't mind owing them. This is the game called love as we've created it. It is not God's love.

God's love gives without needing anything in return. He does not love to get something from us. He does not love because He needs something from us. God loves without looking for something in return. And He loves in such a way that He creates love in us which allows us to love as we have been loved. Christ's birth at the manger, His perfect life, His propitiatory death, and His victorious resurrection were all done knowing that we could not earn such love or repay the debt. This is love. This love is what Christ brought to us, and what He calls us to bring to the world.

Reflection Question:

What are some ways you can love as Christ has loved you during this season?

WEEK 3 - LOVE

DAY 3

Romans 5:6-11

For while we were still weak, at the right time Christ died for the ungodly. [7] For one will scarcely die for a righteous person – though perhaps for a good person one would dare even to die – [8] but God shows his love for us in that while we were still sinners, Christ died for us. [9] Since, therefore, we have now been justified by his blood, much more shall we be saved by him from the wrath of God. [10] For if while we were enemies we were reconciled to God by the death of his Son, much more, now that we are reconciled, shall we be saved by his life. [11] More than that, we also rejoice in God through our Lord Jesus Christ, through whom we have now received reconciliation.

The Child King

The Loving Savior

At Christmas time it's important to think about the manger, Jesus being born, and prophecy being fulfilled, but there is a much bigger story, a much bigger plan! You see, He came, all God and all man, born in a manger to redeem His people. This was the ultimate goal, to reconcile His people unto Himself. This happened through the finished work on the cross. As Romans 5:9-10 says, "Since, therefore, we have now been justified by his blood, much more shall we be saved by him from the wrath of God. For if while we were enemies we were reconciled to God by the death of his Son, much more, now that we are reconciled, shall we be saved by his life."

Enemies of God, redeemed through the work of Christ. Under the law there was a constant need for blood atonement, but now Christ's blood is the ultimate sacrifice. And all of this happened exactly at the time God appointed it to. So, in a season of gift giving, this is His greatest gift! It's a gift that is better than anything we could ever imagine. When you think of Jesus being born this Christmas season, let it be a reminder of the love that He had for you and the reason that He came to this earth.

Reflection Questions:

We give gifts during this season to the people we love. When you do this, does it remind you of the greatest gift, salvation?

How does it make you feel to know that Jesus loved you so much that He laid down His life for you?

WEEK 3 - LOVE

DAY 4

Isaiah 42:8; Matthew 22:37-38

I am the Lord; that is my name;
my glory I give to no other,
nor my praise to carved idols.

And he said to him, "You shall love the Lord your God with all your heart and with all your soul and with all your mind. [38] This is the great and first commandment.

What God Loves Most

We live in a confusing time. Any time love is addressed it is often accompanied by this strange, narcissistic bent that twists and mangles anything that could have been considered love. How we perceive and receive love is so focused on us. My idea of love is usually determined by what someone does for me. Our modern, American Christian culture is rarely different in its definition of love. Jesus loves *me*, died for *me*, left glory for *me*, endured the cross for *me*. *Me. Me. Me.* It is offensive to think that God would do something that glorified something other than His love for *me*. To the degree, that if you were to ask most people in the American church who or what God loves most, the majority would say me or us. But Scriptures and the life of Christ tell a very different story. God does not love us most, and that is the best news ever.

God loves Himself. It may sound awkward to say, but it's true. Jesus proves it. We often think of Jesus' love as being primarily for people. He loved the outcasts and sinners. He loved His enemies from the Cross. But Jesus' love was singularly focused, although so many felt the expression of it. Jesus loved the Father. Christ's perfect obedience in His incarnate life came by His obedience to the Greatest Commandment – loving the Lord alone with His all. God loves God, and He has loved us in Christ that we may learn to love Him most.

Reflection Question:

Think of some ways your love for God needs to focus more on Him and less on you.

WEEK 3 - LOVE

DAY 5

Deuteronomy 6:4-9

Hear, O Israel: The Lord our God, the Lord is one. 5 You shall love the Lord your God with all your heart and with all your soul and with all your might. 6 And these words that I command you today shall be on your heart. 7 You shall teach them diligently to your children, and shall talk of them when you sit in your house, and when you walk by the way, and when you lie down, and when you rise. 8 You shall bind them as a sign on your hand, and they shall be as frontlets between your eyes. 9 You shall write them on the doorposts of your house and on your gates.

The Child King

The Love Which Motivates Us

This passage of scripture has deep meaning for the believer because when asked about the heart of the law Jesus quoted Deuteronomy 6:5. In this moment Jesus reached back into history to show that the most important thing is a total devotion to God out of a heart of love. In this passage we see that love is not just a feeling, but love is commitment expressed in action. It is something that flows from the heart that has been changed by God: to not just say we love Him but to show that we love Him with all our being. This love is not something we hold on to, but we pass down to others as well.

As a father I know that those closest to me are my family. They see the good, the bad, and sometimes the ugly. They are the ones who see my love of God, and they are the ones who see my sin. I'm sure you can relate to that; family always sees everything! In this passage I do not think it is random that God placed family instruction right after a command to love God. If we are to teach others in our normal day-to-day life what it means to love God with our whole being, we cannot fake it with our family. They will know if we truly love God or if God is just one of our many loves. God's command to love requires all of us, not just part of us. If love is commitment expressed in action, it will always show.

Reflection Question:

Today you need to ask yourself, do I love God with my whole being? Then go ask your family what they see in you.

WEEK 3 - LOVE

DAY 6

Leviticus 11:44-45

For I am the Lord your God. Consecrate yourselves therefore, and be holy, for I am holy. You shall not defile yourselves with any swarming thing that crawls on the ground. ⁴⁵ For I am the Lord who brought you up out of the land of Egypt to be your God. You shall therefore be holy, for I am holy."

The Love of Holiness

The command "be holy" has to be one of the most unattainable commands in the Scriptures, especially when you consider the standard of holiness when God says, "Be holy as I am holy." How can we even begin to attempt being holy like God is holy? We have failed to meet the standard of holiness before we've even realized its existence. Our issues with our own failures with holiness are compounded when we consider we will not reach the glory of heaven if we fail at being holy (Hebrews 12:14). We need help to be holy. Thankfully, Christ came to give us the help we needed.

Modern Christians overlook Christ's personal holiness too often. We should love and admire Christ's holiness. We have little trouble, it seems, loving His forgiveness, mercy, compassion, and care for the downcast and marginalized; but we rarely praise Him for His holiness in the ways that we should. Part of the reason is that we feel that Christ is somehow like us in the virtues we've mentioned. We can manufacture the outward expressions of mercy and compassion for the most part, at least when we feel we need to. We cannot manufacture His holiness – His perfection – His righteousness – His purity. The law demands our holiness and His life demands our death so that we might learn to depend on Him. Christ came that we might partake of His holiness as we abide in Him. We need Him to impart His holiness to us. His love for holiness gives us access to the Father we could not approach on our own.

Reflection Question:

List some benefits to loving and understanding Christ's holiness.

WEEK 3 - LOVE

DAY 7

1 John 3:16-18

By this we know love, that he laid down his life for us, and we ought to lay down our lives for the brothers. 17 But if anyone has the world's goods and sees his brother in need, yet closes his heart against him, how does God's love abide in him? 18 Little children, let us not love in word or talk but in deed and in truth.

The Child King

What Love Is

Christ set aside His sovereign position and clothed himself in humanity because of love. Selflessly and willingly He laid down His life for His broken people. He bought us back! This is what true love actually is! The wonderful truth of Christ's love for us should cause us to reciprocate that to the people we come into contact with. At our jobs, schools, and throughout our community. When we see those in need, especially during the Christmas season, we should find great joy in showing the love of Christ.

As Christians, we cannot sit on idle; we are called to minister to those around us that are going through difficult times. We should proclaim the good news of Jesus at every opportunity. But, we have to live out our faith as well. The is a consistent truth throughout scripture, "let us not love in word or talk but in deed and in truth." When we think of the terrible place we were in outside of Christ and the great love that He had for us by laying down His life in our place, we have no choice but to pass that great love along. We display this to the world around us by sacrificing our own desires and humbly serving.

Reflection Question:

How can we follow His example of sacrifice, service, and love?

How would it change our homes and churches if we were humble servants?

WEEK 4 - JOY

DAY 1

Psalm 5:11

But let all who take refuge in you rejoice;
let them ever sing for joy,
and spread your protection over them,
that those who love your name may exult in you.

The Promised Joy

In the Valley of Vision one of the devotionals says,

O CHRIST,
All thy ways of mercy tend to and end in
    my delight.
Thou didst weep, sorrow, suffer that I might rejoice.
For my joy thou hast sent the Comforter,
  multiplied thy promises,
  shown me my future happiness,
  given me a living fountain.
Thou art preparing joy for me and me for joy;
I pray for joy, wait for joy, long for joy;
  give me more than I can hold, desire, or think of.
Measure out to me my times and degrees of joy,
  at my work, business, duties.

The Child King

If I weep at night, give me joy in the morning.
Let me rest in the thought of thy love,
* pardon for sin, my title to heaven,*
* my future unspotted state.*
I am an unworthy recipient of thy grace.
I often disesteem thy blood and slight thy love,
* but can in repentance draw water*
* from the wells of thy joyous forgiveness.*
Let my heart leap towards the eternal sabbath,
* where the work of redemption, sanctification,*
*   preservation, glorification is finished*
*   and perfected for ever,*
* where thou wilt rejoice over me with joy.*
There is no joy like the joy of heaven,
* for in that state are no sad divisions,*
*   unchristian quarrels,*
* contentions, evil designs,*
* weariness, hunger, cold,*
* sadness, sin, suffering,*
* persecutions, toils of duty.*
O healthful place where none are sick!
O happy land where all are kings!
O holy assembly where all are priests!
How free a state where none are servants
* except to thee!*
Bring me speedily to the land of joy.

In this we see the heart of one desiring the promised joy from King Jesus. This is a joy which is present in our lives now and beyond comprehension in the future. It is a joy for all believers in Christ Jesus.

Reflection Question:

Do you long for joy like this writer does in the Valley of Vision?

WEEK 4 - JOY

DAY 2

1 Peter 1:3-5

Blessed be the God and Father of our Lord Jesus Christ! According to his great mercy, he has caused us to be born again to a living hope through the resurrection of Jesus Christ from the dead, 4 to an inheritance that is imperishable, undefiled, and unfading, kept in heaven for you, 5 who by God's power are being guarded through faith for a salvation ready to be revealed in the last time.

Joy in Jesus Alone

Have you ever wondered why some people seem to rejoice more than others about their salvation? I've come to the conclusion that those who rejoice recognize how great salvation truly means. In this passage we see a few things about our salvation which should cause us to have hope. Let me show them to you for a moment.

1. Our Salvation was according to God's mercy and not our worthiness.
2. Our Salvation was accomplished by Jesus and not our works.
3. Our Salvation is sin proof, it's imperishable, we cannot sin our way out of it.
4. Our Salvation is time proof, it's undefiled, we cannot outlast it's effects.
5. Our Salvation is death proof, it's unfading, it's will not end when we do on this earth.
6. Our Salvation is secure by God's Power, He keeps our Salvation through judgment day.

Wow! What amazing truths about our Salvation. Jesus, who came to earth and took on flesh accomplished all of this for us. When we see these truth's it should cause us to rejoice and know what a great Salvation we have because Jesus came to earth!

Reflection Question:

As you look at these six points, does it cause you to rejoice? If so, spend today rejoicing in the truth of your great Salvation.

WEEK 4 - JOY

DAY 3

Psalm 51:8-12

Let me hear joy and gladness;
* let the bones that you have broken rejoice.*
9 Hide your face from my sins,
* and blot out all my iniquities.*
10 Create in me a clean heart, O God,
* and renew a right spirit within me.*
11 Cast me not away from your presence,
* and take not your Holy Spirit from me.*
12 Restore to me the joy of your salvation,
* and uphold me with a willing spirit.*

The Joy of Salvation

It's easy to be distracted by the weight and sorrow of this life. We are constantly struggling with sin in our own flesh. We are constantly confronted with sin in others. And to top it all off, we live in a world corrupted by sin – a world of suffering, loss, war, and disaster. For the regenerate heart, it is difficult at times to celebrate anything knowing that so many bear such heavy burdens. Sometimes, our own burdens are hardest to bear this time of year.

David's lament in Psalm 51 deals primarily with his own sin. He is reeling after his horrendous treatment of Bathsheba and her husband, Uriah. The realities of living in a sinful world weighed heavily on David as he repented of his rebellion against God. He pleads with God to cleanse him – to restore him. The Christian's greatest joy is not that we will escape discomfort, suffering, or death. Instead, we believe we will reach the glory of heaven and be free from sin as we are joined perfectly and eternally with Christ. The *joy of salvation* is found in the promise of eternal life. Christ came to remind us that even though we will have trouble in the world, He has overcome the brokenness and sinfulness of this life (John 16:33). The joy in our salvation is knowing Christ, in His suffering, has redeemed us for Himself.

Reflection Question:

Ask the Lord to renew the joy of your salvation. If you have never experienced His salvation, ask him for mercy. He hears you.

WEEK 4 - JOY

DAY 4

Psalm 27:5-7

For he will hide me in his shelter
*   in the day of trouble;*
he will conceal me under the cover of his tent;
*   he will lift me high upon a rock.*
And now my head shall be lifted up
*   above my enemies all around me,*
and I will offer in his tent
*   sacrifices with shouts of joy;*
I will sing and make melody to the Lord.
Hear, O Lord, when I cry aloud;
*   be gracious to me and answer me!*

Joy in Our Circumstances

As we draw closer and closer to Christmas day things seem to become more and more hectic. Shopping, decorating, Christmas parties, family events, and children's activities fill our calendars. In the middle of it all we can lose sight of what this time of year is all about. We see "Joy" on Christmas decorations and cards throughout this season, but do we honestly think about what joy means?

The Psalmist explains many reasons we can "shout for joy." The Lord conceals, comforts, protects, and is very gracious to us. And in no area has He been more gracious than sending His son, to be born of a virgin, live a sinless life, die in our place, and rise again three days later. For the Christian, this is our great hope! This is true joy! And for this we praise and celebrate Him! There is nothing in this world that can replace or fill the void of the joy that we have in Christ. C.S. Lewis once said, "I sometimes wonder whether all pleasures are not substitutes for joy." Our pleasure is in Christ alone; He is the place we find true joy.

Reflection Question:

What areas of your life do you incorrectly seek joy in?

How can resting in Christ and finding your joy in Him change your outlook each day?

WEEK 4 - JOY

DAY 5

1 Peter 1:6-9

*In this you rejoice, though now for a little while, if necessary, you
have been grieved by various trials, 7 so that the tested genuineness
of your faith – more precious than gold that perishes though it is
tested by fire – may be found to result in praise and glory and
honor at the revelation of Jesus Christ. 8 Though you have not seen
him, you love him. Though you do not now see him, you believe in
him and rejoice with joy that is inexpressible and filled with glory,
9 obtaining the outcome of your faith, the salvation of your souls.*

The Child King

Joy in the Middle of Suffering

Joy is something that is directly tied to faith and not circumstances. In these verses it says that we rejoice in our salvation even when we suffer. We all suffer in this life; you are not alone in this truth. We suffer because we live in a sinful world where sinful decisions are made which affect many people. We suffer because creation has been affected by sin and it groans for the day when Jesus will bring it back to its perfection as it was in the beginning. There is nothing which is not affected by sin, and because of that suffering is a reality in this world – but this text says in the midst of suffering we rejoice in our salvation.

The reason we rejoice is because in the midst of suffering our faith is on display in Christ Jesus. Our faith is on display to our family, our friends, our coworkers, our neighbors, and even people we don't know who may be watching. If our faith is only in good times, what type of faith do we have? What does that say about our joy in Jesus that surpasses circumstances? You see, when we are suffering our faith exposes the glory of God to the people around us, but it also shows that it is real to us. It shows that we truly believe that Jesus is with us now in the suffering and that faith will ultimately be exposed the last day. We can rejoice in our suffering because it speaks the glory of Jesus to those around us but it also speaks to us! In that we can rejoice.

Reflection Question:

Are you rejoicing in your suffering today for God's glory and for your good?

WEEK 4 - JOY

DAY 6

Matthew 28:1-9

Now after the Sabbath, toward the dawn of the first day of the week, Mary Magdalene and the other Mary went to see the tomb. 2 And behold, there was a great earthquake, for an angel of the Lord descended from heaven and came and rolled back the stone and sat on it. 3 His appearance was like lightning, and his clothing white as snow. 4 And for fear of him the guards trembled and became like dead men. 5 But the angel said to the women, "Do not be afraid, for I know that you seek Jesus who was crucified. 6 He is not here, for he has risen, as he said. Come, see the place where he lay. 7 Then go quickly and tell his disciples that he has risen from the dead, and behold, he is going before you to Galilee; there you will see him. See, I have told you." 8 So they departed quickly from the tomb with fear and great joy, and ran to tell his disciples. 9 And behold, Jesus met them and said, "Greetings!" And they came up and took hold of his feet and worshiped him.

He Came to be Raised from the Dead

In our country the word "worship" means many things. To some it means an experience they have at a church, and if they didn't have an experience, they did not worship. To others it means music: when I listen to music and sing along I am worshipping, but outside of music worship does not truly exist. Still to others it means a lifestyle: if I "do good," then I am worshipping. All of these things present an element of truth. On Sundays when God's people gather we do worship, but it's not about an experience if worship takes place. Music does allow us to sing to the Lord, which is a form of worship – but so is reading the Bible, prayer, and taking the Lord's Supper. Our lives are to be ones of worship, but it's not doing good which makes it worship. It's obeying God's commands which makes our lives worship.

The difference is understanding who Jesus is. In this passage the women see Jesus after the resurrection, and they rejoice and fall down in worship. They understood, and the key to worship is knowing the object of their worship, their Messiah, Jesus Christ. When we see Jesus as the clear object of our worship we begin to see what worship is truly all about, a life response to Him and what He accomplished by coming to earth. His greatness goes beyond experiences, music, or doing good. When we see His greatness we rejoice and worship in all the circumstances of our life.

Reflection Question:

Do you see Jesus as the object of your worship in which you rejoice, or do you worship according to your experiences?

WEEK 4 - JOY

DAY 7

Jude 24-25

Now to him who is able to keep you from stumbling and to present you blameless before the presence of his glory with great joy, [25] to the only God, our Savior, through Jesus Christ our Lord, be glory, majesty, dominion, and authority, before all time and now and forever. Amen.

The Father's Great Joy

Great Joy – the Father's response to those who have been reborn – those who were wandering in darkness – those who were dead in their sin but now live by His grace.

Great Joy – the Father's feeling towards those whose sin deserved His wrath – those who were counted His enemies – those who did not want Him as their King before His light shone in their hearts.

Great Joy – towards those for whom Christ became a man – those for whom Christ became a servant – those for whom Christ died the death of the Cross.

Great Joy – towards those who were far off but are now brought near – those who were alienated but are now sons and daughters – those lost but are now found.

The significance of Christ's coming to earth is not simply that we are now able to experience joy that we could not know without Christ, but that the Father Himself takes *great joy* in the salvation of sinners through the work of His Son.

Reflection Question:

How does God's great joy in saving you encourage your walk with Him?

WEEK 5 - CHRIST

Ephesians 1:18-23

having the eyes of your hearts enlightened, that you may know what is the hope to which he has called you, what are the riches of his glorious inheritance in the saints, [19] and what is the immeasurable greatness of his power toward us who believe, according to the working of his great might [20] that he worked in Christ when he raised him from the dead and seated him at his right hand in the heavenly places, [21] far above all rule and authority and power and dominion, and above every name that is named, not only in this age but also in the one to come. [22] And he put all things under his feet and gave him as head over all things to the church, [23] which is his body, the fullness of him who fills all in all.

He is King

The Bible says that Jesus is the name above all. What a great hope we have as Christians in a Savior that conquers all. He has all authority, power, and dominion. Everything is at His feet as He sits at the right hand of the Father ruling and reigning. It's because of Him we receive the inheritance that we do not deserve. For us, this is such a glorious thing that it is almost beyond comprehension.

It is a beautiful story, that from the very beginning God had a plan of redemption. Everything would be made new just like it was, just like it should be. From the Fall, to the first mention of Christ in Genesis 3:15, to the cross when Jesus said, "It is finished," God was working His plan. But that isn't where it all ends. All things will be made new, those that are in Christ will be glorified, and in the new heavens and new earth all will be restored!

Until then, we praise God that He would pay the debt that we owed by laying down His life for us. We praise Him for bringing us into right standing, justified, through the finished work on the cross. Now we walk in obedience to Him so all of the world can see in us the new life we have. And we proclaim the name above all names to the world around us that is in desperate need of a Savior!

Reflection Question:

What does Jesus having all authority, power, and dominion mean and how does it apply to your daily life?

Knowing that you are in Christ should cause you to want to proclaim the good news to the world. How are you doing that?

Why is the Gospel So Important?

There is a word that is crucial to Christianity, a word that if the meaning of this word were removed, Christianity would collapse. That word is *gospel*. The word *gospel* means "the good news," but why is it that important? Why is the gospel so important for Christianity? Let me explain why it's important by looking at four truths.

Truth 1 - God is perfect and set apart.

God created the world, and because He created it, He owns it and can do what He desires with it. He sets the rules. One of God's rules is that for man to be in His presence he must be perfect like God, but if you look at yourself, you know you aren't perfect. Which leads us to truth number two.

Truth 2 - Man isn't perfect; man is sinful.

The reason man isn't perfect like God is because we are sinful and God is not. Man is sinful because in the beginning man broke God's command, and because man broke God's commands all men are sinful and cannot please God and be with God. The Bible calls this being dead in our sins.

This is a problem because this truth has eternal consequences. All men will die. There are no eternal superheroes. Man's life is on the clock, and one day the bell will ring and we will pass from this earth. Since all men will die, what happens after death is incredibly important. Will man be with God, or will man be separated from God? Since we are sinful, all men will be separated from God in Hell instead of being with the perfect God in Heaven. That is bad news, but this is where the good news of the gospel comes in.

The Child King

Truth 3 - God sent Jesus to make dead men alive.

Here is the good news because of the bad news: Since man is sinful and cannot have their sins forgiven by their own works, God sent Jesus to do it for them. Jesus, the Son of God, came to live a sinless life in a sinner's place, the life he cannot live. God sent Jesus to die on the cross and take the punishment for sinners' sin, the punishment they deserve for their sin, and then three days later rise again so dead men could have life.

This is good news! Jesus didn't come to make sinners good. He came to make dead sinners alive.

Truth 4 - Man responds to the good news.

This truth is where man repents of their sin and believes in the first three truths: the truths that God is perfect in all ways, man is totally sinful and dead in their sins, and Jesus came to do what sinful man cannot do, took the punishment that we deserve, and rose from the dead so we can have life.

So we admit we are sinners, we believe that Jesus died for our sins, and we trust in Jesus alone to make us spiritually alive in what He did for sinners.

Now *that* **is why the gospel is important!** If you have not believed in the good news of Jesus, do it today. Admit you are a sinner, believe in the death and resurrection of Jesus, and confess that He is now the Lord of your life.

Printed in Great Britain
by Amazon